D1241380

Books by Howard Moss

POEMS

Second Nature   1968

Finding Them Lost   1965

A Winter Come, A Summer Gone   1960

A Swimmer in the Air   1957

The Toy Fair   1954

The Wound and the Weather   1946

CRITICISM

The Magic Lantern of Marcel Proust   1962

EDITED, WITH AN INTRODUCTION

Keats   1959

The Nonsense Books of Edward Lear   1964

Second Nature

Second Nature

Poems by Howard Moss

New York   Atheneum   *1968*

Grateful acknowledgment is made to the following magazines in which these poems first appeared: THE NEW YORKER (Sands, The Building, Piano Practice, The Bay Stone, The Meeting, Front Street, Particular Beauties, At the Algonquin, The Persistence of Song, Beach Glass, The Vase, Arsenic, Another Life, Still Pond, No More Moving, The Skaters' Waltz, The Dune Wig, The Wars, A Dead Leaf); POETRY (Great Spaces, Going Dutch, The Love Songs of Horatio Alger, Jr.); THE NATION (The Maid's Story); THE TRANSATLANTIC REVIEW (Rusty); and INTRANSIT (Drinks With X).

Library of Congress catalog card number 68–27665
Published simultaneously in Canada by McClelland & Stewart Ltd
Printed by Clarke & Way, New York
Bound by H. Wolff, New York
Designed by Harry Ford
First Edition

For L.W.

Contents

Second Nature

Sands

1

Dry. The wind is parched by the wind.
The stars are machines whose needlepoints
Stab through the throat. Crazed by thirst,
That dog must be killed. Don't cry. Please don't.
It's a waste of water. Yes, I know
The sand is hotter than you can stand,
But, surely, since we have come this far. . . .

2

You'd be surprised
How the body endures
Suffering. What else can it do?
Oh, the mind. That's different. Close your eyes,
And just keep going. Did I ever tell
You stories of Cortez, Ghenghis Khan,
And Hannibal—quite ordinary men?
If we stop now, it will be harder in
The morning. Think of the risk of sun.

3

I'm sorry I said that. Concentrate
On images and dreams, on wanted things
Like streams, springs, and rivulets. . . .
It makes it worse? Think of nothing, then,
But the blood that flows from head to foot
And back, of the brain's banked oxygen,
Of how footfall must follow tread,
If you will it to. You can stand the pain.
Do it for my sake. I ask again.

4

I think the path has become obscure.
The map's inaccurate. I cannot read
The compass because the flashlight's failed,
And we're out of matches. Besides, I think
It was off last time. It's hard to be sure.
Have faith in me. Have faith in me.
Think of all those who have gone before.

5

There must be a country somewhere right now
Of rain, of snow, of golden wind
Where, in the rushes, all that play
Of watery hazards takes the mind.
And that must be the country of joy,
That country that we will never find.
Or perhaps we will. Now we must rest,
Before the sand makes us blind.

6

Only so many miles to go,
And ages in which to do it. So
I like to think. The dog is dead.
I swear
There should be water soon.
We must wait. And wait. The sun's too high.
We'll begin again at the end of day.

7
My darling,
Not to have made it is
To kill, and kill,
And be killed again.
Now, only your body lies
In my bodiless arms,
So dead, so still,

And there is the oasis, up ahead.

The Building

Removed by half a city, not the world,
I see the building you are working in.
It is a winter day. The branches clash
On the few trees that mark the avenue.
If I could go to where I wanted to,
How would I find you? As you were before?
Or are you like the person I've become,
Far into the dark, and far from home?

This winter day was not so dark before
That light was lost that only you could know.
When I go home, and then the dark comes home,
The branches clash along the avenue.
If you could go, I think I'd want you to,
Somewhere the building you'd be working in
Would be a world away, and far from home.
I'm far into the dark when far from you,

And this is something only you could know:
I'm not the person that I was before
You went into the dark. In finding you,
I used to go just where I wanted to.
On the few trees that mark the avenue
The branches clash. It is a winter day.
I see the building you are working in
Removed by half a city, and the world.

Piano Practice

For Frances Dillon Haywood

1

Such splendid icecaps and hard rills, such weights
And counter-weights, I think I scale the heights
When pentatonic Chinese crewmen start
Up in a cold sweat from the bottom of the keyboard
Only to arrive at some snow-stormed valley
To dissolve in steam-holes and vanish out of sight.

2

The left hand's library is dull, the books
All read, though sometimes, going under velvet,
An old upholsterer will spit out tacks,
Turn them into sparks and smartly hurl them
Up and down the loudest bowling alley—
His pressure of effects can last all night.

3

Two bird notes endlessly repeat themselves.
Or are they fish scales—iridescent, hard?
Mica into marble back to mica?
No images in trills. They're formal. Take
Your foot off the pedal. You're in a wood
Near the sea. And every tree and wave is fake.

4

An underwater haircut by Debussy?
Oh, that's too easy. Astringent lotions
Let the swimmer down by easy stages
Down among the flashy soda fountains
Down to the bottom where the light bulbs waver
Down where all the mirrors eat their hearts out.

5

Grammar becoming poetry is what
You're after—say, a rational derangement
Requiring that you forget technique
And concentrate on what is harder like
A fireplace that burns pine needles only,
Before which spills the gore of Persian rugs.

6

A vial of antiseptic meant for Schubert,
One modest, flat meticulous translation
Of Chopin's lightning undercurrent Spanish—
These are the mere necessities of travel.
Someone you must meet is Dr. Czerny.
Then, through him, Domenico Scarlatti.

7

Seizures are occurring. Despite snow-lightning,
The black keys are bent on mountain climbing—
All of it against a doctor's warning.
Soon they're descending like the black dots of
A wirephoto in transmission. An
Erotic black wing hovers up above.

8

Bach is more like opening an ember
And digging hard into the heart of fire.
The heart of fire is another fire.
When it comes to Mozart, just say nothing.
Think of it as milk, and drink it slowly.
Slowly you will taste the cream of angels.

9

This black and white's deceptive. Underneath
The spectrum rages. Did you ever see
The calmest waters quickly come to life
Because a minnow's tinfoil flash in sun
Had rent them suddenly? It came. And went.
We take two thousand takes before we print.

10

Don't try to catch that lion by Rousseau.
Before you wake, he'll eat you up. If you
Should meet the sleeping gypsy, let her sleep.
Tomorrow they'll be gone without a trace,
Half fact and half enigma. Now your hands
Are on the mysteries of the commonplace.

The Bay Stone

The bay's translucency—a thin shellac
Of armor taken off—has taken back
Each chisel stroke of tide, each gallery
The pigments of the world drilled into rock.
This stone is not the stone it used to be.

One membrane still revives it: moisture's touch
Can brush the nerves of fern and fissure back:
Imbedded stress of tiny trees of rust,
Rosettes, and the false sunsets water makes
Before dry air unpaints the stone again.

Because you chose it, your stone is the one
That drops through time to bring all others back
To where anonymously still they drown,
Reflecting vacantly that vacant day,
The day before the bay turned into stone.

Great Spaces

I would worship if I could
Man, woman, child, or dog,
Strip the desert from my back,
Spill an ocean from each eye,
And like those saints who trust to luck

Sit for years under a tree.
I live now in a dirty city
That prowls the sky and is my shade;
Only a low, uneasy light
Gathers there, a light low-keyed

Amid great spaces and great times.
They soon grow smaller. I forget
What months and years once swam through me
As I walked into their great rooms,
Forgotten rooms, forgotten scenes,

And out in space a statue stands
That will not gloss its meaning. Near
Its pedestal, and on its hands
And knees, a figure, wild, unshorn,
Lifts its head to speak. It says,

"Nothing is unwilling to be born."

The Meeting

It never occurred to me, never,
That you were attached to your universe,
Standing on a corner, waiting for a bus,
While the thought-trees grew above your head
And a meadow stretched its rambling sward
All the way up Fifth Avenue.
I was thinking of myself thinking of water,
Of how, each day I went about my job,
I missed one break in the Atlantic Ocean,
Of how I might have been here or there,
Fishing off the coast of Mexico,
Turning the sailboat round the bay,
Or, my chin resting on the concrete edge
Of a swimming pool, I could survey a hill,
The cows' soft blotches stranded in the grass.
Maybe it was that, that last green thing,
That led me into your deepening meadow,
That made me turn among the giant stones
To look one minute into your mind,
To see you running across a field,
The flowers springing up where you had touched.
It was there, I think, we finally met.

Front Street

1

The moon's little skullcap,
Dry divinity,
Has brought all color
Into question:
What is your skin now—
Lime or gray?
It has a kind of phosphorescent shine.
Fluorescent? Is that what I mean?
There are no words to describe it.

2

That greasy tug
Might be a spy,
That flashing lens
A trained binocular.
A death rattle has obsessed the tree
And a strangling sound the harbor water,
Which keeps saying, "Don't count on me!"—
As if we were such fools
To count on it ever!

3

I'm sorry the sick palms look so rundown,
That Front Street, which used to be so gay,
Seems like the street of a plague-ridden town—
Empty, apprehensive, dirty.
Do not go down the steps into the boat.
A storm is coming.
Can't you hear the wind?
Do you think I enjoy being arbitrary?
Do what I say.
Or else we'd better say goodbye right now.

4

Why did I bring you to Front Street? Because
The boats are here,
In case we have to make a quick get-away.
All right. Call it irrational fear.
The Jews in Germany, one year before
They saw the handwriting on the wall,
Would have thought you mad
If you'd told them where
They'd all end up. Think of Oedipus
A second before the blind seer opened his mouth.
No. We're not going back.
We're going some place. Anywhere.
Somewhere we can be, temporarily, safe.

5

You think nature's a left-handed compliment?
A French one's more like it;
I could have told you, twenty years ago,
It's a dirty dig. Think of a time,
Five years, or one,
When people weren't at each other's throats.
Everywhere there are miles of files
With our names typed in them, yours and mine.
The point is to be invisible
Or blinding, nothing in between—
Famous or anonymous . . .
But it's much too late for people like us.

6
O.k. O.k. We'll go back to the house.
A false alarm?
What a child you are!
Remember when we get back into town,
And the sun's shining, oh, so bright,
And everything seems so right, so fine,
So permanent,
Front Street will be waiting at our backs.

Particular Beauties

Whether it was a particular beauty
Stirred the tearfall from the eyelid's rim,
Rinsing the world once more with self,
Was it not there the general peered,
Thousand-eyed, down from the peak
In the last of all imaginary sunsets?
The light divided in half, the half
Divided again in half, the way
Zeno's paradox makes nothing move
Because an infinity of points between
Target and arrow, though never seen,
Exists. And there is snow in a capsule,
A solid floor of individual
Flakes that, shaken, settle in a field—
Parachutists growing where the grass,
One moment before, was only natural.
I am speaking now of the diminishment
Or enhancement of enchanted objects,
Of how they turn into nothingness
Or burnish the imagination:
A fire at the bottom of the sea,
For instance, or a mind in space
Thinking its way into science fiction,
Or, inside the skull, a little world
Clinging, about to be thrown away—
Miraculous lint under a bell.

At the Algonquin

He sat at the Algonquin, smoking a cigar.
A coffin of a clock bonged out the time.
She was ten minutes late. But in that time,
He puffed the blue eternity of his cigar.

Did she love him still? His youth was gone.
Humiliation's toad, with its blank stares
Squatted on his conscience. When they went upstairs,
Some version of them both would soon be gone.

Before that, though, drinks, dinner, and a play—
The whole demanding, dull expense account
You paid these days for things of no account.
Whatever love may be, it's not child's play.

Slowly she walked toward him. God, we are
Unnatural animals! The scent of roses
Filled the room above the carpet's roses,
And, getting up, he said, "Ah, *there* you are!"

The Persistence of Song

Although it is not yet evening,
The secretaries have changed their frocks
As if it were time for dancing,
And locked up in the scholars' books
There is a kind of rejoicing,
There is a kind of singing
That even the dark stone canyon makes
As though all fountains were going
At once, and the color flowed from bricks
In one wild, lit upsurging.

What is the weather doing?
And who arrived on a scallop shell
With the smell of the sea this morning?
—Creating a small upheaval
High above the scaffolding
By saying, "All will be well.
There is a kind of rejoicing."

Is there a kind of rejoicing
In saying, "All will be well?"
High above the scaffolding,
Creating a small upheaval,
The smell of the sea this morning
Arrived on a scallop shell.
What was the weather doing

In one wild, lit upsurging?
At once, the color flowed from bricks
As though all fountains were going,
And even the dark stone canyon makes
Here a kind of singing,
And there a kind of rejoicing,
And locked up in the scholars' books
There is a time for dancing
When the secretaries have changed their frocks,
And though it is not yet evening,

There is the persistence of song.

Beach Glass

Mr. Calava rises at five
A.M., the first on the beach, but not
Because he's crazy about the sea.
He's crazy about beach glass. He has
Two thousand pieces
At the latest count.
An industry of idleness,
He's a connoisseur of broken glass.

Sucked candy bits as hard as lava,
The shards are no longer sharp and come
In every shape and every color—
The commonest are white and brown:
Harder to find are blue and green;
Amber is rare; yellow rarer;
And red the rarest of all. The sea's

A glass-blower who blasts to bits
Coca-Cola and Waterford,
Venetian as well as Baccarat,
And has carefully combed its five-and-ten
For anything made of glass. It isn't
Fussy. It knows that everything
Will be pared down in the end:
Milk of magnesia bottles honed
To sky-blue icy filaments,
And smoky cordial bottles from
Brazil—sunglasses of an eclipse.

Mr. Calava's kaleidoscopes
Are kept in apothecary jars,
As if the sea were a pharmacy
Of lozenges and doled them out
Without a prescription, especially
For Mr. Calava, who firmly believes
The best things in life are free.

But what the sea has relinquished it
Has relinquished only in part. You know
How childish it is in its irony.
The jig-saw puzzle is here. But then
Its missing pieces are still in the sea.
Not all the king's horses and all the king's men
Could ever put it together again,
Though—chip by chip
And bit by bit—

Rouault could make a King of it.

The Vase

Before the summer flowers fell,
I set the vase of autumn out,
And in that spare receptacle
Pure form alone exists without

The feasibility of bloom
And takes the sky into its depth,
A skylight in a living room
Whose walls are slowly papered with

Dead leaves on dead, until those walls—
The curved sides of the vase—rise up,
Revealing endless vestibules,
Those alleys where each shadowgraph

Is still the shadow of a vase
No longer there. I wake to no
Paint boxes stacked against the skies
To hear the rainpipe drip of snow.

Arsenic

They will be telling you soon who you are,
The importunate, slovenly younger thinkers—
But only because they are young. From afar,
You may hear certain familiar voices,
Romantic but growing increasingly dim,
Express themselves in some thirty sounds
Out of a possible twenty thousand;
The terraces will be swinging in place
With their few discordant violins, the lamps
Hissing with gas, the smell of an old
Shoebox suddenly tainting the wharf—
Or could the sky's incredible liquor
Be responsible for the odor of
A set of ancient mah-jongg tiles
You found in your mother's closet once?
What are they doing here on the coast?
They are lusterless now from disuse and the sun.

> *"I have taken a sufficient dose and still*
> *Feel nothing, a slight burning sensation*
> *But no smell of garlic, the telltale sign.*
> *Strange. And several seconds have passed.*
> *No pain. But for those who follow, I note*
> *That the phone will appear farther away . . ."*

Now they will tell you your favorite words,
Symbols gone sickly with use—such as
Gull   blue   ocean   house—
Are no longer possible. And they're right.
You *have* been a bit of a fool. You have
Been feeling your way
When you should have gone straight
To the heart of the matter. Which is what?
To have looked humiliation full
In the face instead of walking around
It, like a dog chained to a pole . . .

For instance, a letter arrived this week,
Saying

> *"You're not expressing yourself.*
> *It's hard to know who you are."*

These facts
Are relevant:
I have never killed.
I have loved three times—
Possibly four—
I have two suits
I will never wear.
The mornings are bad,
But by evening I'm
Myself again.

Do you know me now, Miss Mandarin?
You of the scented, mauve-lined page
Who tell me that you were once a nun

But now, when a sailor stalks the streets,
You feel the old magic welling up,
The thing most of all you're afraid to lose?
Don't tell me *you're* the one who wrote
Three hundred times on a warehouse wall
"Don't knock love!" If so, I shake
Your hand still blue from chalk. . . .

3 THE THIRD LETTER

But there it is. One word
Used up already. Blue.
And here's another, thinly disguised:

Meanwhile the sea, a hundred yards away,
Already bored with its literary career,
Is beating itself up, again, again,
And, sick of the moon's attentions every night,
Is carving a sandbar farther out
Behind which it hopes to draw its skirts
And thus avoid the shore's vulgar display.
It's deluded, of course. It isn't very bright.
But it's beautiful. Which, around here, is right.

Now I am going back to the house
For a drink. From the upper porch, I see
A gull go by on the steadiest wings
You ever saw. If a scavenger's
That gorgeous, what will they say of me?
There's something to be said for everything.
For garbage, for instance, in this case.

"I've been meaning to write much sooner but
Something has kept me from saying just
What I wanted to . . . Are you well? Does J.
Still wake each night and need comforting?
I think, perhaps, that the lack of love,
Yes, love . . . I feel you no longer
Love, sincerely, with a thousand thoughts . . ."

Starlight, dear walk, when this view is
Nothing but emptied space and snow,
When no foot breaks its silences,
What faces, guests will then arrive
Frantic with their reasons to live?

Another Life

There might be the quibble of birds and the swag
Of a river and a distantly belled
Altar of animals, softly spoken;
Certainly cattail, sumac, and fern
Would rise from the marshes nearby, revealed
In forms too perfect to envy trees—
Not trying for larger and larger keepsakes.

Cryptic and subtle green, hedgerows
Hiding mysterious deer, the start
Of a rabbit, as if towers and clouds
Had suddenly shadowed an open field—
These would be the events of the day,
Life having narrowed down to please
Natural hungers and thirsts, the grass
Thick at our feet, and, above our heads,
The stars, their firework anemones.

What shall I say of the house? Or you?
Only industrious ghosts would know
How lazily cropping up the view
Would make the impossible possible;
Nothing but weekdays would blankly graze
On time's oblivious pastures, free
At last of motive and thought, and we,
Becoming ourselves so naturally,
Would never say, looking up at the sky,
Another life is shining in the sky.

The Maid's Story

Between her leaving Cobh
And putting the kettle on
Each morning on the stove,
Twenty springs had gone.

A slow flutter of nerves
Told her the slow truth:
There was to be no love
In heaven or on earth.

She never could put the losses
In words, never could say—
When they asked, "What's the matter?"—
What was the matter. They

Were patient and impatient
Like the city she stared at.
She was lint in the clothes closet.
She was dust under the rug.

She stayed that way for years,
In between loss and loss;
Each night, she dreamed of a house
That was hers. It never was.

Then less and less mattered,
Each day was just each day.
Finally nothing mattered,
She opened her mouth to say.

Going Dutch

Two gloves, a lipstick, and a corduroy
Bag, a saucer filling up with butts. . . .
A check will soon be coming to their joy,
That joy they nourish on their separate cots.
They halve the bill and take a flying walk
Up Fifth. A rip of blue. And then it's dark.

A bar. The old songs. Who remembers now
That dated country of a five o'clock
Piano tinkling out its moving, shallow
Tune that gives the heart its little knock?
The sentimental is so trivial,
One gin erases it or brings it back.

They're home now. Separately. She sprays her hair,
Puts down her cigarette, afraid of fire,
While he takes down a book he's read before;
Starting it, he starts to think of her—
The dream: Her figure floating up the stair,
His floating down, not going anywhere.

2

" 'Judas.' 'Three.' Those words are in my head,"
She said, and drew a circle in the ash—
Cigarette ash in which a sybil read
On the tabletop with all its dirty wash.
How many years had passed between the two?
Fifteen? Twenty? Nothing seemed to change:
Her flint of beauty staggered on one shoe,
His crooked insight wandered out of range.
"But am I menaced? And by whom?" he asked.

The sybil spoke in wonders and in dreads:
"Beware the envious. Stay quiet. Work.
In six months, maybe you'll be safe." The reds
And whites of a checkered cloth were shaken free;
A piece of old French bread, a glass of wine
Were put back on the table. Close to three,
They sat as if their money were their time.

3
Strange, the validity of the past,
As if the sound of distant traffic
Slowly floated up to consciousness,
A small jazz combo at the bottom of the ocean
Disturbed by somebody's auxiliary motor,
Or the thunder of the sea as the waves pass.

Still Pond, No More Moving

They have taken the maps and spread them out
And parted from each other,
Have slipped the rivers into their veins
And pocketed the sandy beaches,
Have gone walking through slow trains
Across where the Mississippi bends,
Have gone in even slower freighters
Down the irregular coastlines—
The inlet's curve, the island's nest
Lure them along a dotted line
Back or forward, forward or back,
And some have settled at an address.

Above them all the same sky
Shapes the mountain or meets the shore,
And some—now undecided why
They chose one or the other—stare
Out of a crooked window from
A ramshackle cabin on a dune
At the slow rollers coming in,
The sheets hung out on a clothesline,
While the children's disparate cries
Rise up from the hard shore,
And someone is looking up
Wishing that he were where
The pines soar to the mountaintop
Or stop at the snowline.

2

Is it water they want, water,
The sea changingly in,
Or, cool to the tilted diver
Ringed round by quarry walls,
The stills of deep water
That make him weightless, blind,
As he soars back to the beginning,
That spring without a mind?
Or the highest mountain places
Where the sudden shaded lake
Refreshes the eye because
No two lakes are alike?

And sometimes by its absence—
Or by its opposite—
Water is strangely felt:
In New Mexico, appearance
Conceived as existence springs
Forward into the distance
In vanishing parallels
Of skylines of lighted cliffs
That race up to the hills;
The desert, its own mirage,
Breaks in wave on wave
Between the bloodied mountains
At the running out of day,
And when the sun says it is
Life and death at once,
There, in the few trees,
Water stands up to dance.

3

And some are far out at sea.
The horizon is growing dark.
Someone is taking a walk
On the deck of a dipping hull—
Or the deck awash in a storm—
Barely holding on—
While some at the ship's bar
Sit while an arm extends
Their gin and their caviar,
And find with the first sip
The seepage of doubt begin:
Oh, what did I come for?
What am I doing here?
Supposing the lights went off
And we stopped right where we are?

4

Who is painting the barn door?
Who is painting the painter there,
Summer after summer,
The summer plucked from the year?
But there is that one summer
When old age, like a stick
Thrown for a retriever
Who does not bring it back,
Keeps drifting farther out
Till it's no longer seen—
One mountainside slides down,
One city street slams shut,
A piece of the sea is gone.

Is it Hythe or Rockaway?
Or the Puerto Rican waves
That roll in in the same way?
Or Rosarita Beach
Where the sulphur of the sand
Is marked by the horse's hoof,
And the Moorish hotel stands,
A white elephant, aloof,
Where once the gamblers jammed
The tables, and now one goes
Into almost empty rooms
And the four guitarists come
To the table to serenade?

5

I know some landscapes where
Intensity comes late,
And, deepening in light,
Brings such an inner peace
That floating by in the gold
The world is half dissolved
And the last birds cry farewell
To the day and the shadows seem
To lean on the trees in the wood.

And others where morning comes
Spun out on a crystal web,
And innocence is abroad
And drinks in the new-made world,
And nothing appears to be
Violent or amiss,
And silence would be a tree,
Except that the wind is.

6

Someone is bitterly thinking
The innermost's not said:
Where is the great theme?
Whoever saw the world
At once and saw it whole?
In New England now,
Here where the water is,
Here where the red barn
Is an advocate of hills,
Time rigs up famous shapes,
The white whales, the white ships,
Yet in summer's lapse
The drunken sea bards come
To lounge on all its Capes.

The Skaters' Waltz

I'd like to hear The Skaters' Waltz again
And see Vienna on my TV set
With pictures of the King and Queen I love.
What is it makes them all so dear to me?
The skaters' icy skill, the dancers' verve?
I do not know if that's a polished floor
Or a pond so brightly lit that, in its glare,
Inverted on the brilliant ice, the world
Is hanging like a crystal chandelier
Ready to be dropped or be drawn up
In one quick graceful gesture. But I fear
When it goes up or down that so will we.
That's why on winter nights, and summer, too,
The thing above all else I like to do
Is listen to The Skaters' Waltz again,
Because as long as all the dancers turn,
I think they'll play it on and on and on . . .

Rusty

Hot *what* in the hot rod just sped by
The lights, direct grass? Violences?
Caught in the stucco: words and lines
Scrawled on the toilet walls, or scrawled
In Spanish on a white wall (but that was
In another country.) That was Mind,
Rusty's mind, made up of trips
To sex and back, but in the comic strips.
"I never minded what they said," he said,
"I never minded it at all," he said,
And raced through shantytown and out of it.
Was he the self-destructive principle?
What killed him? Rusty! What killed *you*?
Those languid mornings at the A. and P.,
The lettuce leaves breathing the country,
The dirt that clung to every carrot root,
The sawdust like a circus underfoot,
And all for money, money, money . . .?
"Oh, not for money," Rusty would say,
"Oh, no, no, no! I did it all for love."

The Dune Wig

Ice had hollowed out the dunes, dead trees
Thrust roots into the air along that coast
Where all was lost for trees, where all was lost
For you and me; the desolation there
Brought winter into heat: the glacial frost
The rocks made visible, the dune's dry wigs—
The still-felt analogues of old affairs.
The bay weed's thick Sargasso webbed us in
So that each footstep, taking time, made time
A slower crepitation at the rim.

Bay gravel shook inside a tambourine.
I watched you walking out to see the dead
Horseshoe crab, its limp and twisted meat
Hanging from its shell, a floating mine.
Something like a sunburst rocked my head,
Burning in to touch me—as you had.
Since love is of the body, since your hand
Is still imprinted on my skin, I bear
The mark of Scandinavian countries
That were the gold dune-grasses of your hair.

Drinks with X

"Yes, Paris is lovely from a balcony,"
The woman says. The woman in black.
I look down at the Rue de Wolfe. There are
Several imposing hotels and one
Café where a hunchbacked man writes notes.
The waitress is fanning away the flies.
It's August. Most of the French are away.
A few people walk up and down the streets.

She says, "I have my exotic birds,
My pianos tinkling with absence, cakes
Yet to be eaten by queens, blue seas
Hung up in sunny courtyards to dry,
And slides made of ice with love details
Still thought to be pornographic by
The vulgar—those who have never loved.
I, who have nibbled at everything,

Develop the negatives of the heart
At a glance. The heart, oh, the heart," she cries.
"Naturally, cruelty comes into it
Since we are all egotistical,
But let me assure you again I will
Be waiting patiently at the end
When, waking from summer's sluggish dream,
You crash into snow. Just think of me

As old disappointment's youngest child,
Modest but sly, with ten thousand veils
To screen the Soul from Reality—
The thing is to say goodbye to the past,
Then cultivate the remains. Who's *here*?
Is always the question one should ask.
Too many tears have been shed in vain,
And for what? Half-loaves of love or fame. . . .

When I think of the possibilities!
Get out a map or walk five blocks
Away from your usual daylight haunts.
(Only a fool would revise the night!)
Civilization and nature both
Can offer such startling illusory gifts:
The sunset having its heart attack,
The telephone wires' encephalogram.

And now, I'm afraid we must part. Goodbye.
Thank you so much for the splendid view,
Which combines the banal and spectacular.
I would have preferred so much more to be
At home, engrossed in a mystery—
And aren't we *all* engrossed in one?—
Or worse, smoking myself to death,
Ha ha, in front of my tiny TV. . . .

One last word. I'd avoid the beach
If I were you, and not just because
We're not as young as we used to be.
How true it is that the old clichés
Say the most! How's that? My tiny TV?
Oh, yes, of course we have them here.
And *there*, too. But I must. . . . Bonjour.
And don't forget: I'll be seeing you."

The Wars

How can I tell you of the terrible cries
Never sounded, of the nerves that fail,
Not in jungle warfare or a southern jail,
But in some botched affair where two people sit
Quite calmly under a blood-red lamp
In a Chinese restaurant, a ludicrous swamp
Of affection, fear drowning in the amber
Tea when no word comes to mind
To stand for the blood already spilled,
For rejection, denial, for all those years
Of damage done in the polite wars?

And what do I know of the terrible cries
That are really sounded on the real hill
Where the soldiers sweat in the Asian night
And the Asians sweat where the soldiers flail
The murderous grass, and the peasants reel
Back in a rain of gasoline,
And the shells come home and the bombs come down
Quite calmly under a blood-red moon
Not far from China, and the young are killed,
Mere numerals in the casualties
Of this year's war, and the war of years?

He stands with a knife in the Daily News.
They are snaking their way into the hills.
She is walking up Broadway to hurt again.
They are fleeing under a hail of shells.
He is taking her neck into his hands.
A human seed squats in the dark.
She is scalding the baby in the bath.
He feels the bullet enter his skin.
She spits in the face of the riot squad.
They are sitting down, they are opening wounds.

The Love Songs of Horatio Alger, Jr.

I

About to fall in love
With someone I won't remember
A decade from now, I tie
The knot in my best bowtie
And stumble down twenty stairs
And cross ten streets of rain,
And then it all starts again . . .

You take this old address:
Somebody lived here once.
I couldn't even guess
The name, the face, but once

I raced up twenty stairs
And nobody was in,
And I walked slowly down.

Is it the rain, the rain
That makes me feel again
What I thought I couldn't feel?
The sound of the rainfall,
Hardly a sound at all.

2

Walking the wet macadam for
The alterations of the night,
I dream the dream of in between:
The sad and indecisive street
Where crippled children skate at five,
Where their wax crutches melt in light.

I see the madman's eyes insist
On taking children home to bed
To weave of them his hair and skin,
His nest, his love, his window scene,
Until the crow at the violet hour
Comes with black songs in his throat
To sing of coincidence and murder.

3

I cherish most the libidinous moment
When, striving done, with a sensual comment,
I ransom back my golden will.
The city of stars within my skull
Stops circling. When its sky is still,
That mouth I kissed, those eyes that teared
Lie dead, and I'm King Lear out-Leared,
For though my storm was all light verse,
Its lines still shook my universe.

Concrete ribbons shine in the dark
Among the stilted lakes and trees
Slick with reflected light, the fake
Cuts, montages, and bad re-takes
Of rainy Saturday movie scenes.
My heart that once leaked gold I now
Hold back, my mistresses disappear
Into the quicksand of the years,
But I shall join them when I shed
These dollar signs that are my eyes,
This ticker tape that is my brain,
When, with my wallet full, I fall
Into the biggest deal of all.

A Dead Leaf

Today, the first dead leaf in the hall
Is surprised, taking on its second nature,
To find that trees are forms of furniture;
The earliest message to arrive from winter,
It's too far gone, indoors or out,
To eat the sun or drink the water,
And I, I am more desperate than ever,
Reading the memoirs that Madame Blank
Keeps sending on in thick installments.
Twelve publishers have firmly declined. . .
(Thank God! For I am thinly disguised
As yet another form of furniture:
My name is Harrod—a character
Who at one point rather stupidly remarks,
"Only a Fool could love King Lear.")
Madame would hate these opening lines;
She is against both cadence and meter.

Armories, windows,
Days and weeks
Of peering out, then drawing back—
Is there enough artillery
To blast the gossips of this block?
Paranoia is a borderline
Without a country on either side.
That fortress of brownstones across the way
Is money talking
With nothing to say.

Rectitude and impropriety!
I have given them both up,
And settled for a sleazy mysticism,
Befuddled rain and poisoned mist;
Sometimes I'm so depressed I think
It's *life* that's the anesthetist.
But then I wake quite sane, as if
A bicycle race were about to start:
I'm in the park, the sun is bright,
Water ravishes the eye, and soon
I've won the race, I've made my mark!
Then, once again, the telephone
Is my one lifeline out of the dark.

I'm sick of being obsessed by B.
Whose muffled cryptograms grow hoarse
Explaining themselves, outwitting me.
Does that mean this? Does this mean that?
Temperamental unclarity!

This week, drinks and dinner with M.
Lunch with L. Dinner with P.
A party for C.'s new Argentine.
Handel on Thursday. A *vernissage*.
Next week, drinks and dinner with M.
Tuesday I think I'll watch TV.

To retire from it all! To sit and sit
In a wheelchair, old, in Central Park,
Only a lens that drinks the sun,
Or on a bench in southern France,
The first cassis at four o'clock. . . .

August was green, November brown.
Someday soon I'll awake to see
The world go white from head to toe,
A tablecloth at first, and then
A slab of pockmarked travertine—

The first snow.

Howard Moss

Howard Moss was born in New York City in
1922. He is the author of five previous collections
of poetry, and a critical book, *The Magic Lantern
of Marcel Proust*. He has written several plays, the
most recent of which is *The Palace at 4 A.M.*
which was given a staged reading at The
Playwrights' Unit in April, 1968. Another play,
The Oedipus Mah-Jongg Scandal was produced by
the Cooperative Theatre Club in May of the same
year. A new book of criticism will be published
in the spring of 1969. He is the poetry editor of
The New Yorker.

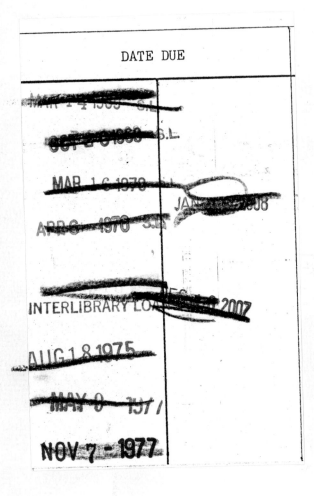